The Scrum Guide™	3
The Purpose of the Scrum Guide	3
Definition of Scrum	3
Uses of Scrum	4
Scrum Theory	4
Transparency	5
Inspection	5
Adaptation	5
Scrum Values	5
The Scrum Team	5
The Product Owner	7
The Development Team	7
Development Team Size	8
The Scrum Master	8
Scrum Master Service to the Product Owner	8
Scrum Master Service to the Development Team	8
Scrum Master Service to the Organization	9
Scrum Events	9
The Sprint	9
Cancelling a Sprint	10
Sprint Planning	10
Topic One: What can be done this Sprint?	10
Topic Two: how will the chosen work get done?	11
Sprint Goal	11
Daily Scrum	11
Sprint Review	12
Sprint Retrospective	13
Scrum Artifacts	13
Product Backlog	13
Monitoring Progress Toward Goals	14
Sprint Backlog	14
Monitoring Sprint Progress	15
Increment	15
Transparency	15
Definition of "Done"	16

- Scrum in action! 16
  - Inspect & adapt 17
  - Agile Development and Scrum 17
- Scrum Basics (Scrum 101) 18
  - How Scrum Works 18
    - The Product Backlog 18
  - The Team 18
    - Product Owner 18
    - Scrum Master 18
    - The Team 18
  - The Sprint 18
    - Sprint Planning 18
    - Daily Standup 18
    - Sprint Review 19
    - Sprint Retrospective 19
- Scrum in action 20
  - The Product Backlog 20
  - Sprint Planning 21
  - Daily Standup 22
  - Updating Sprint Backlog & Sprint Burndown Chart 23
  - Product Backlog Refinement 24
  - Ending the Sprint 24
  - Sprint Review 24
  - The Sprint Retrospective 25
  - Updating Release Backlog & Burndown Chart 25
  - Starting the Next Sprint 25
  - Release Sprint 25
  - Release Planning & Initial Product Backlog Refinement 26
    - Application or Product Focus 27
  - Common Challenges 27
  - Distributed, Outsourced Scrum 27
  - Distributed Team Models 28

The Scrum Guide™

This latest version of the Scrum Guide is the November 2017 version available **as a PDF** from Scrum.Org (https://www.scrumguides.org)

The Purpose of the Scrum Guide

Scrum is a framework for developing, delivering, and sustaining complex products. This guide aims to support the Scrum Guide and provide a definition consists of Scrum's roles, events, artifacts, and the rules that bind them together.

Ken Schwaber and Jeff Sutherland developed Scrum in 2009 and the Scrum Guide is written and provided by them. Together, they maintain and update it on a regular basis.

Definition of Scrum

Scrum (n): A framework within which people can address complex adaptive problems, while productively and creatively delivering products of the highest possible value.

Scrum is:
- Lightweight
- Simple to understand
- Difficult to master

Scrum is a process framework (*note it is not a process*) that has been used to manage work on complex products since the early 1990s. Scrum is not a process, technique, or definitive method. Rather, it is a framework within which you can employ various processes and techniques. Scrum makes clear the relative efficacy of your product management and work techniques so that you can continuously improve the product, the team, and the working environment.

The Scrum framework consists of Scrum Teams and their associated roles, events, artifacts, and rules. Each component within the framework serves a specific purpose and is essential to Scrum's success and usage.

The rules of Scrum bind together the roles, events, and artifacts, governing the relationships and interaction between them. The rules of Scrum are described throughout the body of this document.

Specific tactics for using the Scrum framework vary and are described elsewhere.

Uses of Scrum

Scrum was initially developed for managing and developing products. Starting in the early 1990s, Scrum has been used extensively, worldwide, to:

1. Research and identify viable markets, technologies, and product capabilities;
2. Develop products and enhancements;
3. Release products and enhancements, as frequently as many times per day;
4. Develop and sustain Cloud (online, secure, on-demand) and other operational environments for product use; and,
5. Sustain and renew products.

Scrum has been used to develop software, hardware, embedded software, networks of interacting function, autonomous vehicles, schools, government, marketing, managing the operation of organizations and almost everything we use in our daily lives, as individuals and societies.

As technology, market, and environmental complexities and their interactions have rapidly increased, Scrum's utility in dealing with complexity is proven daily.

Scrum proved especially effective in iterative and incremental knowledge transfer. Scrum is now widely used for products, services, and the management of the parent organization.

The essence of Scrum is a small team of people. The individual team is highly flexible and adaptive. These strengths continue operating in single, several, many, and networks of teams that develop, release, operate and sustain the work and work products of thousands of people. They collaborate and interoperate through sophisticated development architectures and target release environments.

When the words "develop" and "development" are used in the Scrum Guide, they refer to complex work, such as those types identified above.

Scrum Theory

Scrum is founded on empirical process control theory, or empiricism. Empiricism asserts that knowledge comes from experience and making decisions based on what is known. Scrum employs an iterative, incremental approach to optimize predictability and control risk. Three pillars uphold every implementation of empirical process control: transparency, inspection, and adaptation.

Scrum is an agile method designed to add energy, focus, clarity, and transparency to project planning and implementation. Today, Scrum is used in small, mid-sized and large software corporations all over the world. It is being used in more and more areas beyond software.

Properly implemented, Scrum will:
- Increase speed of development
- Align individual and corporate objectives
- Create a culture driven by performance
- Support shareholder value creation
- Achieve stable and consistent communication of performance at all levels

Transparency

Significant aspects of the process must be visible to those responsible for the outcome. Transparency requires those aspects be defined by a common standard so observers share a common understanding of what is being seen.

For example:
- A common language referring to the process must be shared by all participants; and,
- Those performing the work and those inspecting the resulting increment must share a common definition of "Done".

Inspection

Scrum users must frequently inspect Scrum artifacts and progress toward a Sprint Goal to detect undesirable variances. Their inspection should not be so frequent that inspection gets in the way of the work. Inspections are most beneficial when diligently performed by skilled inspectors at the point of work.

Adaptation

If an inspector determines that one or more aspects of a process deviate outside acceptable limits, and that the resulting product will be unacceptable, the process or the material being processed must be adjusted. An adjustment must be made as soon as possible to minimize further deviation.

Scrum prescribes four formal events for inspection and adaptation, as described in the Scrum Events section of this document:
- Sprint Planning
- Daily Scrum
- Sprint Review
- Sprint Retrospective

Scrum Values

When the values of commitment, courage, focus, openness and respect are embodied and lived by the Scrum Team, the Scrum pillars of transparency, inspection, and adaptation come to life and build trust for everyone. The Scrum Team members learn and explore those values as they work with the Scrum events, roles and artifacts.

Successful use of Scrum depends on people becoming more proficient in living these five values. People personally commit to achieving the goals of the Scrum Team. The Scrum Team members have courage to do the right thing and work on tough problems. Everyone focuses on the work of the Sprint and the goals of the Scrum Team. The Scrum Team and its stakeholders agree to be open about all the work and the challenges with performing the work. Scrum Team members respect each other to be capable, independent people.

The Scrum Team

The Scrum Team consists of a Product Owner, the Development Team, and a Scrum Master. Scrum Teams are self-organizing and cross-functional. Self-organizing teams choose how best to accomplish their work, rather than being directed by others outside the team. Cross-functional teams have all competencies needed to accomplish the work without depending on others not part of the team. The team model in Scrum is designed to optimize flexibility, creativity, and productivity. The Scrum Team has proven itself to be increasingly effective for all the earlier stated uses, and any complex work.

Scrum Teams deliver products iteratively and incrementally, maximizing opportunities for feedback. Incremental deliveries of "Done" product ensure a potentially useful version of working product is always available.

The Product Owner

The Product Owner is responsible for maximizing the value of the product resulting from work of the Development Team. How this is done may vary widely across organizations, Scrum Teams, and individuals.

The Product Owner is the sole person responsible for managing the Product Backlog.

Product Backlog management includes:
- Clearly expressing Product Backlog items;
- Ordering the items in the Product Backlog to best achieve goals and missions;
- Optimizing the value of the work the Development Team performs;
- Ensuring that the Product Backlog is visible, transparent, and clear to all, and shows what the Scrum Team will work on next; and,
- Ensuring the Development Team understands items in the Product Backlog to the level needed.

The Product Owner may do the above work, or have the Development Team do it. However, the Product Owner remains accountable.

The Product Owner is one person, not a committee. The Product Owner may represent the desires of a committee in the Product Backlog, but those wanting to change a Product Backlog item's priority must address the Product Owner.

For the Product Owner to succeed, the entire organization must respect his or her decisions. The Product Owner's decisions are visible in the content and ordering of the Product Backlog. No one can force the Development Team to work from a different set of requirements.

The Development Team

The Development Team consists of professionals who do the work of delivering a potentially releasable Increment of "Done" product at the end of each Sprint. A "Done" increment is required at the Sprint Review. Only members of the Development Team create the Increment.

Development Teams are structured and empowered by the organization to organize and manage their own work. The resulting synergy optimizes the Development Team's overall efficiency and effectiveness.

Development Teams have the following characteristics:
- They are self-organizing. No one (not even the Scrum Master) tells the Development Team how to turn Product Backlog into Increments of potentially releasable functionality;
- Development Teams are cross-functional, with all the skills as a team necessary to create a product Increment;
- Scrum recognizes no titles for Development Team members, regardless of the work being performed by the person;
- Scrum recognizes no sub-teams in the Development Team, regardless of domains that need to be addressed like testing, architecture, operations, or business analysis; and,
- Individual Development Team members may have specialized skills and areas of focus, but accountability belongs to the Development Team as a whole.

Development Team Size

Optimal Development Team size is small enough to remain nimble and large enough to complete significant work within a Sprint. Fewer than three Development Team members decrease interaction and results in smaller productivity gains.

Smaller Development Teams may encounter skill constraints during the Sprint, causing the Development Team to be unable to deliver a potentially releasable Increment. Having more than nine members requires too much coordination.

Large Development Teams generate too much complexity for an empirical process to be useful. The Product Owner and Scrum Master roles are not included in this count unless they are also executing the work of the Sprint Backlog.

The Scrum Master

The Scrum Master is responsible for promoting and supporting Scrum as defined in the Scrum Guide. Scrum Masters do this by helping everyone understand Scrum theory, practices, rules, and values.

The Scrum Master is a servant-leader for the Scrum Team. The Scrum Master helps those outside the Scrum Team understand which of their interactions with the Scrum Team are helpful and which aren't. The Scrum Master helps everyone change these interactions to maximize the value created by the Scrum Team.

Scrum Master Service to the Product Owner

The Scrum Master serves the Product Owner in several ways, including:
- Ensuring that goals, scope, and product domain are understood by everyone on the Scrum Team as well as possible;
- Finding techniques for effective Product Backlog management;
- Helping the Scrum Team understand the need for clear and concise Product Backlog items;
- Understanding product planning in an empirical environment;
- Ensuring the Product Owner knows how to arrange the Product Backlog to maximize value;
- Understanding and practicing agility; and,
- Facilitating Scrum events as requested or needed.

Scrum Master Service to the Development Team

- The Scrum Master serves the Development Team in several ways, including:
- Coaching the Development Team in self-organization and cross-functionality;
- Helping the Development Team to create high-value products;
- Removing impediments to the Development Team's progress;
- Facilitating Scrum events as requested or needed; and,
- Coaching the Development Team in organizational environments in which Scrum is not yet fully adopted and understood.

Scrum Master Service to the Organization

The Scrum Master serves the organization in several ways, including:
- Leading and coaching the organization in its Scrum adoption;
- Planning Scrum implementations within the organization;
- Helping employees and stakeholders understand and enact Scrum and empirical product development;
- Causing change that increases the productivity of the Scrum Team; and,
- Working with other Scrum Masters to increase the effectiveness of the application of Scrum in the organization.

Scrum Events

Prescribed events are used in Scrum to create regularity and to minimize the need for meetings not defined in Scrum. All events are time-boxed events, such that every event has a maximum duration. Once a Sprint begins, its duration is fixed and cannot be shortened or lengthened. The remaining events may end whenever the purpose of the event is achieved, ensuring an appropriate amount of time is spent without allowing waste in the process.

Other than the Sprint itself, which is a container for all other events, each event in Scrum is a formal opportunity to inspect and adapt something.

These events are specifically designed to enable critical transparency and inspection. Failure to include any of these events results in reduced transparency and is a lost opportunity to inspect and adapt.

The Sprint

The heart of Scrum is a Sprint, a time-box of one month or less during which a "Done", useable, and potentially releasable product Increment is created. Sprints have consistent durations throughout a development effort. A new Sprint starts immediately after the conclusion of the previous Sprint.

Sprints contain and consist of the Sprint Planning, Daily Scrums, the development work, the Sprint Review, and the Sprint Retrospective.

During the Sprint:
- No changes are made that would endanger the Sprint Goal;
- Quality goals do not decrease; and,
- Scope may be clarified and re-negotiated between the Product Owner and Development Team as more is learned.

Each Sprint may be considered a project with no more than a one-month horizon. Like projects, Sprints are used to accomplish something. Each Sprint has a goal of what is to be built, a design and flexible plan that will guide building it, the work, and the resultant product increment.

Sprints are limited to one calendar month. When a Sprint's horizon is too long the definition of what is being built may change, complexity may rise, and risk may increase. Sprints enable predictability by ensuring inspection and adaptation of progress toward a Sprint Goal at least every calendar month. Sprints also limit risk to one calendar month of cost.

Cancelling a Sprint

A Sprint can be cancelled before the Sprint time-box is over. Only the Product Owner has the authority to cancel the Sprint, although he or she may do so under influence from the stakeholders, the Development Team, or the Scrum Master.

A Sprint would be cancelled if the Sprint Goal becomes obsolete. This might occur if the company changes direction or if market or technology conditions change. In general, a Sprint should be cancelled if it no longer makes sense given the circumstances. But, due to the short duration of Sprints, cancellation rarely makes sense.

When a Sprint is cancelled, any completed and "Done" Product Backlog items are reviewed. If part of the work is potentially releasable, the Product Owner typically accepts it. All incomplete Product Backlog Items are re-estimated and put back on the Product Backlog. The work done on them depreciates quickly and must be frequently re-estimated.

Sprint cancellations consume resources, since everyone regroups in another Sprint Planning to start another Sprint. Sprint cancellations are often traumatic to the Scrum Team, and are very uncommon.

Sprint Planning

The work to be performed in the Sprint is planned at the Sprint Planning. This plan is created by the collaborative work of the entire Scrum Team.

Sprint Planning is time-boxed to a maximum of eight hours for a one-month Sprint. For shorter Sprints, the event is usually shorter. The Scrum Master ensures that the event takes place and that attendants understand its purpose. The Scrum Master teaches the Scrum Team to keep it within the time-box.

Sprint Planning answers the following:
- What can be delivered in the Increment resulting from the upcoming Sprint?
- How will the work needed to deliver the Increment be achieved?

Topic One: What can be done this Sprint?

The Development Team works to forecast the functionality that will be developed during the Sprint. The Product Owner discusses the objective that the Sprint should achieve and the Product Backlog items that, if completed in the Sprint, would achieve the Sprint Goal. The entire Scrum Team collaborates on understanding the work of the Sprint.

The input to this meeting is the Product Backlog, the latest product Increment, projected capacity of the Development Team during the Sprint, and past performance of the Development Team.

The number of items selected from the Product Backlog for the Sprint is solely up to the Development Team. Only the Development Team can assess what it can accomplish over the upcoming Sprint.
During Sprint Planning the Scrum Team also crafts a Sprint Goal. The Sprint Goal is an objective that will be met within the Sprint through the implementation of the Product Backlog, and it provides guidance to the Development Team on why it is building the Increment.

Topic Two: how will the chosen work get done?

Having set the Sprint Goal and selected the Product Backlog items for the Sprint, the Development Team decides how it will build this functionality into a "Done" product Increment during the Sprint. The Product Backlog items selected for this Sprint plus the plan for delivering them is called the Sprint Backlog.

The Development Team usually starts by designing the system and the work needed to convert the Product Backlog into a working product Increment. Work may be of varying size, or estimated effort. However, enough work is planned during Sprint Planning for the Development Team to forecast what it believes it can do in the upcoming Sprint. Work planned for the first days of the Sprint by the Development Team is decomposed by the end of this meeting, often to units of one day or less. The Development Team self-organizes to undertake the work in the Sprint Backlog, both during Sprint Planning and as needed throughout the Sprint.

The Product Owner can help to clarify the selected Product Backlog items and make trade-offs. If the Development Team determines it has too much or too little work, it may renegotiate the selected Product Backlog items with the Product Owner. The Development Team may also invite other people to attend to provide technical or domain advice.

By the end of the Sprint Planning, the Development Team should be able to explain to the Product Owner and Scrum Master how it intends to work as a self-organizing team to accomplish the Sprint Goal and create the anticipated Increment.

Sprint Goal

The Sprint Goal is an objective set for the Sprint that can be met through the implementation of Product Backlog. It provides guidance to the Development Team on why it is building the Increment. It is created during the Sprint Planning meeting. The Sprint Goal gives the

Development Team some flexibility regarding the functionality implemented within the Sprint. The selected Product Backlog items deliver one coherent function, which can be the Sprint Goal. The Sprint Goal can be any other coherence that causes the Development Team to work together rather than on separate initiatives.

As the Development Team works, it keeps the Sprint Goal in mind. In order to satisfy the Sprint Goal, it implements functionality and technology. If the work turns out to be different than the Development Team expected, they collaborate with the Product Owner to negotiate the scope of Sprint Backlog within the Sprint.

Daily Scrum

The Daily Scrum is a 15-minute time-boxed event for the Development Team. The Daily Scrum is held every day of the Sprint. At it, the Development Team plans work for the next 24 hours. This optimizes team collaboration and performance by inspecting the work since the last Daily Scrum and forecasting upcoming Sprint work. The Daily Scrum is held at the same time and place each day to reduce complexity.

The Development Team uses the Daily Scrum to inspect progress toward the Sprint Goal and to inspect how progress is trending toward completing the work in the Sprint Backlog. The Daily Scrum optimizes the probability that the Development Team will meet the Sprint Goal. Every day, the Development Team should understand how it intends to work together as a self-organizing team to accomplish the Sprint Goal and create the anticipated Increment by the end of the Sprint.

The structure of the meeting is set by the Development Team and can be conducted in different ways if it focuses on progress toward the Sprint Goal. Some Development Teams will use questions, some will be more discussion based.

Here is an example of what might be used:
- What did I do yesterday that helped the Development Team meet the Sprint Goal?
- What will I do today to help the Development Team meet the Sprint Goal?
- Do I see any impediment that prevents me or the Development Team from meeting the Sprint Goal?

The Development Team or team members often meet immediately after the Daily Scrum for detailed discussions, or to adapt, or replan, the rest of the Sprint's work.

The Scrum Master ensures that the Development Team has the meeting, but the Development Team is responsible for conducting the Daily Scrum. The Scrum Master teaches the Development Team to keep the Daily Scrum within the 15-minute time-box.

The Daily Scrum is an internal meeting for the Development Team. If others are present, the Scrum Master ensures that they do not disrupt the meeting.

Daily Scrums improve communications, eliminate other meetings, identify impediments to development for removal, highlight and promote quick decision-making, and improve the Development Team's level of knowledge. This is a key inspect and adapt meeting.

Sprint Review

A Sprint Review is held at the end of the Sprint to inspect the Increment and adapt the Product Backlog if needed. During the Sprint Review, the Scrum Team and stakeholders collaborate about what was done in the Sprint. Based on that and any changes to the Product Backlog during the Sprint, attendees collaborate on the next things that could be done to optimize value.

This is an informal meeting, not a status meeting, and the presentation of the Increment is intended to elicit feedback and foster collaboration.

This is at most a four-hour meeting for one-month Sprints. For shorter Sprints, the event is usually shorter. The Scrum Master ensures that the event takes place and that attendees understand its purpose. The Scrum Master teaches everyone involved to keep it within the time-box.

The Sprint Review includes the following elements:
- Attendees include the Scrum Team and key stakeholders invited by the Product Owner;
- The Product Owner explains what Product Backlog items have been "Done" and what has not been "Done";
- The Development Team discusses what went well during the Sprint, what problems it ran into, and how those problems were solved;
- The Development Team demonstrates the work that it has "Done" and answers questions about the Increment;
- The Product Owner discusses the Product Backlog as it stands. He or she projects likely target and delivery dates based on progress to date (if needed);
- The entire group collaborates on what to do next, so that the Sprint Review provides valuable input to subsequent Sprint Planning;
- Review of how the marketplace or potential use of the product might have changed what is the most valuable thing to do next; and,
- Review of the timeline, budget, potential capabilities, and marketplace for the next anticipated releases of functionality or capability of the product.

- The result of the Sprint Review is a revised Product Backlog that defines the probable Product Backlog items for the next Sprint. The Product Backlog may also be adjusted overall to meet new opportunities.

Sprint Retrospective

The Sprint Retrospective is an opportunity for the Scrum Team to inspect itself and create a plan for improvements to be enacted during the next Sprint.

The Sprint Retrospective occurs after the Sprint Review and prior to the next Sprint Planning.

This is at most a three-hour meeting for one-month Sprints. For shorter Sprints, the event is usually shorter. The Scrum Master ensures that the event takes place and that attendants understand its purpose.

The Scrum Master ensures that the meeting is positive and productive. The Scrum Master teaches all to keep it within the time-box. The Scrum Master participates as a peer team member in the meeting from the accountability over the Scrum process.

The purpose of the Sprint Retrospective is to:
- Inspect how the last Sprint went with regards to people, relationships, process, and tools;
- Identify and order the major items that went well and potential improvements; and,
- Create a plan for implementing improvements to the way the Scrum Team does its work.

The Scrum Master encourages the Scrum Team to improve, within the Scrum process framework, its development process and practices to make it more effective and enjoyable for the next Sprint. During each Sprint Retrospective, the Scrum Team plans ways to increase product quality by improving work processes or adapting the definition of "Done", if appropriate and not in conflict with product or organizational standards.

By the end of the Sprint Retrospective, the Scrum Team should have identified improvements that it will implement in the next Sprint. Implementing these improvements in the next Sprint is the adaptation to the inspection of the Scrum Team itself. Although improvements may be implemented at any time, the Sprint Retrospective provides a formal opportunity to focus on inspection and adaptation.

Scrum Artifacts

Scrum's artifacts represent work or value to provide transparency and opportunities for inspection and adaptation. Artifacts defined by Scrum are specifically designed to maximize transparency of key information so that everybody has the same understanding of the artifact.

Product Backlog

The Product Backlog is an ordered list of everything that is known to be needed in the product. It is the single source of requirements for any changes to be made to the product. The Product Owner is responsible for the Product Backlog, including its content, availability, and ordering.

A Product Backlog is never complete. The earliest development of it lays out the initially known and best-understood requirements. The Product Backlog evolves as the product and the environment in which it will be used evolves. The Product Backlog is dynamic; it constantly changes to identify what the product needs to be appropriate, competitive, and useful. If a product exists, its Product Backlog also exists.

The Product Backlog lists all features, functions, requirements, enhancements, and fixes that constitute the changes to be made to the product in future releases. Product Backlog items have the attributes of a description, order, estimate, and value. Product Backlog items often include test descriptions that will prove its completeness when "Done".

As a product is used and gains value, and the marketplace provides feedback, the Product Backlog becomes a larger and more exhaustive list. Requirements never stop changing, so a Product Backlog is a living artifact. Changes in business requirements, market conditions, or technology may cause changes in the Product Backlog.

Multiple Scrum Teams often work together on the same product. One Product Backlog is used to describe the upcoming work on the product. A Product Backlog attribute that groups items may then be employed.

Product Backlog refinement is the act of adding detail, estimates, and order to items in the Product Backlog. This is an ongoing process in which the Product Owner and the Development Team collaborate on the details of Product Backlog items. During Product Backlog refinement, items are reviewed and revised. The Scrum Team decides how and when refinement is done.

Refinement usually consumes no more than 10% of the capacity of the Development Team. However, Product Backlog items can be updated at any time by the Product Owner or at the Product Owner's discretion.

Higher ordered Product Backlog items are usually clearer and more detailed than lower ordered ones. More precise estimates are made based on the greater clarity and increased detail; the lower the order, the less detail. Product Backlog items that will occupy the Development Team for the upcoming Sprint are refined so that any one item can reasonably be "Done" within the Sprint time-box. Product Backlog items that can be "Done" by the Development Team within one Sprint are deemed "Ready" for selection in a Sprint Planning. Product Backlog items usually acquire this degree of transparency through the above described refining activities.

The Development Team is responsible for all estimates. The Product Owner may influence the Development Team by helping it understand and select trade-offs, but the people who will perform the work make the final estimate.

Monitoring Progress Toward Goals

At any point in time, the total work remaining to reach a goal can be summed. The Product Owner tracks this total work remaining at least every Sprint Review. The Product Owner compares this amount with work remaining at previous Sprint Reviews to assess progress toward completing projected work by the desired time for the goal. This information is made transparent to all stakeholders.

Various projective practices upon trending have been used to forecast progress, like burn-downs, burn-ups, or cumulative flows. These have proven useful. However, these do not replace the importance of empiricism. In complex environments, what will happen is unknown. Only what has already happened may be used for forward-looking decision-making.

Sprint Backlog

The Sprint Backlog is the set of Product Backlog items selected for the Sprint, plus a plan for delivering the product Increment and realizing the Sprint Goal. The Sprint Backlog is a forecast by the Development Team about what functionality will be in the next Increment and the work needed to deliver that functionality into a "Done" Increment.

The Sprint Backlog makes visible all the work that the Development Team identifies as necessary to meet the Sprint Goal. To ensure continuous improvement, it includes at least one high priority process improvement identified in the previous Retrospective meeting.

The Sprint Backlog is a plan with enough detail that changes in progress can be understood in the Daily Scrum. The Development Team modifies the Sprint Backlog throughout the Sprint, and the Sprint Backlog emerges during the Sprint. This emergence occurs as the Development Team works through the plan and learns more about the work needed to achieve the Sprint Goal.

As new work is required, the Development Team adds it to the Sprint Backlog. As work is performed or completed, the estimated remaining work is updated. When elements of the plan are deemed unnecessary, they are removed. Only the Development Team can change its Sprint Backlog during a Sprint. The Sprint Backlog is a highly visible, real-time picture of the work that the Development Team plans to accomplish during the Sprint, and it belongs solely to the Development Team.

Monitoring Sprint Progress

At any point in time in a Sprint, the total work remaining in the Sprint Backlog can be summed. The Development Team tracks this total work remaining at least for every Daily Scrum to project the likelihood of achieving the Sprint Goal. By tracking the remaining work throughout the Sprint, the Development Team can manage its progress.

Increment

The Increment is the sum of all the Product Backlog items completed during a Sprint and the value of the increments of all previous Sprints. At the end of a Sprint, the new Increment must be "Done," which means it must be in useable condition and meet the Scrum Team's definition of "Done". An increment is a body of inspectable, done work that supports empiricism at the end of the Sprint. The increment is a step toward a vision or goal. The increment must be in useable condition regardless of whether the Product Owner decides to release it.

Transparency

Scrum relies on transparency. Decisions to optimize value and control risk are made based on the perceived state of the artifacts. To the extent that transparency is complete, these decisions have a sound basis. To the extent that the artifacts are incompletely transparent, these decisions can be flawed, value may diminish and risk may increase.

The Scrum Master must work with the Product Owner, Development Team, and other involved parties to understand if the artifacts are completely transparent. There are practices for coping with incomplete transparency; the Scrum Master must help everyone apply the most appropriate practices in the absence of complete transparency. A Scrum Master can detect incomplete transparency by inspecting the artifacts, sensing patterns, listening closely to what is being said, and detecting differences between expected and real results.

The Scrum Master's job is to work with the Scrum Team and the organization to increase the transparency of the artifacts. This work usually involves learning, convincing, and change. Transparency doesn't occur overnight, but is a path.

Definition of "Done"

When a Product Backlog item or an Increment is described as "Done", everyone must understand what "Done" means. Although this may vary significantly per Scrum Team, members must have a shared understanding of what it means for work to be complete, to ensure transparency. This is the definition of "Done" for the Scrum Team and is used to assess when work is complete on the product Increment.

The same definition guides the Development Team in knowing how many Product Backlog items it can select during a Sprint Planning. The purpose of each Sprint is to deliver Increments of potentially releasable functionality that adhere to the Scrum Team's current definition of "Done".

Development Teams deliver an Increment of product functionality every Sprint. This Increment is useable, so a Product Owner may choose to immediately release it. If the definition of "Done" for an increment *is* part of the conventions, standards or guidelines of the development organization, all Scrum Teams must follow it as a minimum.

If "Done" for an increment is *not* a convention of the development organization, the Development Team of the Scrum Team must define a definition of "Done" appropriate for the product. If there are multiple Scrum Teams working on the system or product release, the Development Teams on all the Scrum Teams must mutually define the definition of "Done".

Each Increment is additive to all prior Increments and thoroughly tested, ensuring that all Increments work together.

As Scrum Teams mature, it is expected that their definitions of "Done" will expand to include more stringent criteria for higher quality. New definitions, as used, may uncover work to be done in previously "Done" increments. Any one product or system should have a definition of "Done" that is a standard for any work done on it.

Scrum in action!

Scrum is an iterative, incremental framework for projects and product or application development.

Scrum structures development in cycles of work called Sprints. These iterations are less than one month in length, and usually measured in weeks. Sprints take place one after the other. The Sprints are of fixed duration – they end on a specific date whether the work has been completed or not, and are never extended. Hence, they are said to be time boxed.

At the beginning of each Sprint, a cross-functional team selects items (customer requirements) from a prioritized list. They commit to complete the items by the end of the Sprint. During the Sprint, the chosen items do not change. Every day the Team gathers briefly to replan its work to optimize the likelihood of meeting commitments.

At the end of the Sprint, the team reviews the Sprint with stakeholders, and demonstrates what they have built. People obtain feedback that can be incorporated in the next Sprint.

Inspect & adapt

Scrum emphasizes a working product at the end of the Sprint that is really "done". In the case of software, this means code that is:

- Integrated
- Fully Tested
- Potentially Shippable

A major theme in Scrum is "inspect and adapt." Since development inevitably involves learning, innovation, and surprises, Scrum emphasizes taking a short step of development, inspecting both the resulting product and the efficacy of current practices, and then adapting the product goals and process practices. Repeat forever.

Agile Development and Scrum

Scrum is, as the reader supposedly knows, an agile method. The agile family of development methods evolved from the old and well-known iterative and incremental lifecycle approaches. They were born out of a belief that an approach more grounded in human reality and the product development reality of learning, innovation, and change –
would yield better results.

Agile principles emphasize building working software that people can get hands on quickly, versus spending a lot of time writing specifications up front. Agile development focuses on cross- functional teams empowered to make decisions, versus big hierarchies and compartmentalization by function. It also focuses on rapid iteration, with continuous customer input along the way. Often when people learn about agile development or Scrum, there's a glimmer of recognition – it sounds a lot like back in the start-up days

"when we just did it."

Scrum was strongly influenced by a 1986 Harvard Business Review article on the practices associated with successful product development groups by Professors Takeuchi and Nonaka. in this paper the term "Scrum" was introduced, relating successful development to the game of Rugby in which a self-organizing (self- managing) team moves together down the field of product development. The first Scrum team was created at Easel Corporation in 1993 by Dr. Jeff Sutherland (the author of this manual) and the Scrum framework was
formalized in 1995 by Jeff and Ken Schwaber.

Scrum Basics (Scrum 101)

How Scrum Works

The Product Backlog

A Scrum project is driven by a product vision created by the Product Owner, and expressed in the Product Backlog.

The Product Backlog is a prioritized list of what's required, ranked in order of value to the customer or business, with the highest value items at the top of the list. The Product Backlog evolves over the lifetime of the project, and items are continuously added, removed or reprioritized.

The Team

Product Owner

Takes the inputs of what the product should be and translates them into a product vision or a Product Backlog.

Scrum Master

Does whatever it takes to make the Scrum Team successful, such as removing organizational impediments, facilitating meetings, acting as a gatekeeper so no one unnecessary interrupts the team's work.

The Team

Makes the product envisioned by the Product Owner.

The Sprint

Scrum structures product development in cycles of work called Sprints, iterations of work that are typically 1–4 weeks in length. The Sprints are of fixed duration and end on a specific date whether the work has been completed or not; they are never extended.

Sprint Planning

At the beginning of each Sprint, the Sprint Planning Meeting takes place. The Product Owner and Team (with facilitation from the ScrumMaster) reviews the Product Backlog, discuss the goals and context for the items, and the Team selects the items from the Product Backlog to commit to complete by the end of the Sprint, starting at the top of the Product Backlog. Each item selected from the Product Backlog is designed and then broken down to a set of granulated steps. This list of backlog items is recorded in a document called the Sprint Backlog.

Daily Standup

Once the Sprint has started, the Team engages in another of the key Scrum practices: The Daily Stand-Up Meeting. This is a short (15 minutes) meeting that happens every workday at an appointed time. Everyone on the team attends. At this meeting, the information needed to inspect progress is presented. This information may result in re-planning and further discussions immediately after the Daily Standup.

Sprint Review

After the Sprint ends, there is the Sprint Review, where the Scrum Team and stakeholders inspect what was done during the Sprint, discuss it, and figure out what to do next.

Present at this meeting are the Product Owner, Team Members, and ScrumMaster, plus customers, stakeholders, experts, executives, and anyone else interested.

Sprint Retrospective

Following the Sprint Review, the team gets together for the Sprint Retrospective which is an opportunity for the team to discuss what's working and what's not working, and agree on changes to try.

Scrum in action

Initiating a Scrum project is not hard, as long as one takes one step at a time, and makes sure that everyone feels included.

The Product Backlog

The first step in Scrum is for the Product Owner to articulate the product vision.

Eventually, this evolves into the refined and prioritized list of features, the Product Backlog.

This backlog exists and evolves over the lifetime of the product; it is the product road map. At any point, the Product Backlog is the single, definitive view of "everything that could be done by the team ever, in order of priority". Only a single Product Backlog exists; this means the Product Owner is required to make prioritization decisions across the entire spectrum.

The Product Backlog includes a variety of items, primarily new customer features ("enable all users to place book in shopping cart"), but also engineering improvement goals ("rework the transaction processing module to make it scalable"), exploratory or research work ("investigate solutions for speeding up credit card validation"), performance and security requirements, and, possibly, known defects ("diagnose and fix the order processing script errors"), if there are only a few problems. (A system with many defects usually has a separate defect tracking system.) Many people like to articulate the requirements in terms of "user stories" - concise, clear descriptions of the functionality in terms of its value to the end user of the product. In more demanding environments, such as FDA life critical applications, Use Cases are often used.

The subset of the Product Backlog that is intended for the current release is known as the Release Backlog, and in general, this portion is the primary focus of the Product Owner.

The Product Backlog is continuously updated by the Product Owner to reflect changes in the needs of the customer, new ideas or insights, moves by the competition, technical hurdles that appear, and so forth.

The team provides the Product Owner with estimates of the effort required for each item on the Product Backlog. In addition, the Product Owner is responsible for assigning a business value estimate to each individual item. This is often an unfamiliar practice for a Product Owner.

With the two estimates (effort and value) and perhaps with additional risk estimates, the Product Owner prioritizes the backlog (actually, usually just the Release Backlog subset) to maximize ROI (choosing items of high value with low effort) or secondarily, to reduce some major risk.

As will be seen, these effort and value estimates may be refreshed each Sprint as people learn; consequently, this is a continuous re-prioritization activity and the Product Backlog is ever evolving.

Scrum does not mandate the form of estimates in the Product Backlog, but it is common to use relative estimates expressed as "points" rather than absolute units of effort such as person-weeks.

Over time, a team tracks how many relative points they implement each Sprint; for example, averaging 26 points per Sprint.

With this information they can project a release date to complete all features, or how many features will likely be completed by a date. Standard deviations around the average points will indicate least likely and most likely possibilities. The number of points completed per Sprint is called the velocity of the team. A realistic release plan is always based on the velocity of the team.

The items in the Product Backlog can vary significantly in size, effort and complexity. Larger ones are broken into smaller items during the Product Backlog Refinement workshop or the Sprint Planning Meeting, and smaller ones may be consolidated.

Sprint Planning

The Sprint Planning Meeting opens the Sprint. It is divided into two distinct sub-meetings, the first of which is called Sprint Planning Part One.

In Sprint Planning Part One, the Product Owner and Team (with facilitation from the Scrum Master) review the high-priority items in the Product Backlog that the Product Owner is interested in implementing this Sprint. They discuss the goals and context for these high-priority items on the Product Backlog, providing the Team with insight into the Product Owner's thinking. The Product Owner and Team also review the "Definition of Done" that all items must meet, such as, "Done means coded to standards, reviewed, implemented with unit test-driven development (TDD), tested with 100 percent test automation, integrated, and documented." This definition of "done" ensures transparency and quality fit for the purpose of the product and organization.

Part One focuses on understanding what the Product Owner wants.

According to the rules of Scrum, at the end of Part One the (always busy) Product Owner may leave although they must be available (for example, by phone) during the next meeting.

However, they are welcome to attend Part Two...

Sprint Planning Part Two, often referred to as Sprint Refinement, focuses on detailed task planning for how to implement the items that the team decides to take on. The Team selects the items from the Product Backlog they commit to complete by the end of the Sprint, starting at the top of the Product Backlog (in others words, starting with the items that are the highest priority for the Product Owner) and working down the list in order.

While the Product Owner does not have control over how much the team commits to, he or she knows that the items the team is committing to are drawn from the top of the Product Backlog – in other words, the items that he or she has rated as most important.

The team has the authority to also select items from further down the list in consultation with the Product Owner; this usually happens when the team and Product Owner realize that something of lower priority fits easily and appropriately with the high priority items.

The Sprint Planning Meeting should be time boxed to four hours for a four-week Sprint and two hours for a two-week Sprint. In order to do this, the team must help the Product Owner by estimating the size of stories before the Sprint Planning meeting – the team is making a serious commitment to complete the work, and this commitment requires careful thought to be successful. A Team bases its commitments on its past velocities.

If a Team is new, new to the technology or domain, it may not have reliable, stable velocities until it has worked together for three or four Sprints. In making its commitment, the Team factors in any vacations, new organizational demands, and other items that may reduce its past velocity.

Once the Team capacity available is determined, the Team starts with the first item on the Product Backlog – in other words, the Product Owner's highest priority item – and working together, breaks it down into individual stories, which are recorded in a document called the Sprint Backlog (see below).

As mentioned, the Product Owner must be available during Part Two (such as via the phone) so that clarifications and decisions regarding alternative approaches is possible. The team will move sequentially down the Product Backlog in this way, until it's used up all its capacity. At the end of the meeting, the team will have produced a list of tasks with estimates (typically in hours or fractions of a day). The list is a starting point, but more tasks will emerge as the Team addresses each Product Backlog item during the Sprint. The Team will work on a technical design that will be implemented using Sprint Backlog tasks. The team choses the ordering of Sprint Backlog tasks to maximize the velocity of production and quality of "done" functionality.

Scrum encourages multi-skilled workers, rather than only "working to job title" such as a "tester" only doing testing. In other words, team members "go to where the work is" and help out as possible. If there are many testing tasks, then all Team members may help. This does not imply that everyone is a generalist; no doubt some people are especially skilled in testing (and so on) but Team members work together and learn new skills from each other. Pairing has proven a valuable approach to sharing knowledge.

All that said, there are rare times when a Team member may do a particular task because it would take far too long or be impossible for others to learn – perhaps he or she is the only person with the artistic skill to draw pictures. Other Team members could not draw a "stick man" if their lives depended on it. In this rare case – and if it is not rare and not getting rarer as the Team learns, there is something wrong – it may be necessary to ask if the total planned drawing tasks that must be done by this certain Team member are feasible within the short Sprint.

One of the pillars of Scrum is that once the Team makes its commitment, any additions or changes must be deferred until the next Sprint. This means that if halfway through the Sprint the Product Owner decides there is a new item he or she would like the Team to work on, he cannot make the change until the start of the next Sprint. If an external circumstance appears that significantly changes priorities, and means the Team would be wasting its time if it continued working, the Product Owner or the team can terminate the Sprint. The Team stops, and a new Sprint Planning meeting initiates a new Sprint. The disruption of doing this is usually great; this serves as a disincentive for the Product Owner or team to resort to this dramatic decision.

By following these Scrum rules the Product Owner gains two things. First, he or she has the confidence of knowing the Team has made a commitment to complete a realistic and clear set of tasks they have chosen. Over time a Team can become quite skilled at choosing and delivering on a realistic commitment. Second, the Product Owner gets to make whatever changes he or she likes to the Product Backlog before the start of the next Sprint. At that point, additions, deletions, modifications, and re-prioritizations are all possible and acceptable. While the Product Owner is not able to make changes to the selected items under development during the current Sprint, he or she is only one Sprint's duration or less away from making any changes. Gone is the stigma around change – change of direction, change of requirements, or just plain changing your mind – and it may be for this reason that Product

Owners are usually as enthusiastic about Scrum as anyone and the Scrum Master may need to "monitor and control" this enthusiasm.

Daily Standup

Once the Sprint has started, the Team engages in another of the key Scrum practices: The Daily Standup. This is a short (15 minutes or less) meeting that happens every workday at an appointed time and place. Everyone on the Team attends. To keep it brief, it is recommended that everyone remain standing. It is the Team's opportunity to talk to each other and inspect each other's progress and obstacles. In the Daily Standup, one by one, each member of the team reports three (and only three) things to the other members of the team:

- What did I do yesterday that helped the Development Team meet the Sprint Goal?
- What will I do today to help the Development Team meet the Sprint Goal?
- Do I see any impediment that prevents me or the Development Team from meeting the Sprint Goal?

It must be noted that the Daily Standup is not a status meeting or a report to a manager; it is a time for a self-organizing Team to share with each other what is going on, to help it coordinate its work and optimize its likelihood of meeting its commitments. Someone makes note of the blocks, and the Scrum Master is responsible for helping team members resolve them. There is no chit-chat during the Daily Standup, only reporting answers to the three questions; if discussion is required it takes place immediately after the Daily Standup in a follow-up meeting, although in Scrum no one is required to attend this. This follow-up meeting is a common event where the Team adapts to the information they heard in the Daily Standup: in other words, another inspect and adapt cycle.

It is generally recommended not to have managers or others in positions of perceived authority attend the Daily Standup. This risks making the Team feel "monitored" – under pressure to report major progress every day (an unrealistic expectation), and inhibited about reporting problems – and it tends to undermine the Team's self-management, and invite micromanagement. It would be more useful for a stakeholder to instead reach out to the team following the meeting, and offer to help with any blocks that are slowing the Team's progress.

Updating Sprint Backlog & Sprint Burndown Chart

Every day, the Team members update their estimate of the amount of time remaining to complete their current task in the Sprint Backlog. Following this update, someone adds up the points remaining for the Team as a whole, and plots it on the Sprint Burndown Chart.

This graph shows, each day, a new estimate of how much work (measured in relative points) remains until the Team's tasks are finished. Ideally, this is a downward sloping graph that is on a trajectory to reach "zero effort remaining" by the last day of the Sprint. Hence it is called a burndown chart. And while sometimes it looks good, often it does not; this is the reality of product development. The important thing is that it shows the Team their progress towards their goal, not in terms of how much time was spent in the past (an irrelevant fact in terms of progress), but in terms of how much work remains in the future – what separates the Team from their goal.

If the burndown line is not tracking downwards towards completion by mid-Sprint, the team needs to execute the Scrum Emergency

Procedure:
1. Change the approach to the work or remove impediments to increase velocity.
2. Get help by having someone outside the team take some of the backlog.
3. Reduce the scope of work.
4. Abort the Sprint.

It is important that the Scrum Master coach the Team to take action early rather than drifting into Sprint failure. Some Scrum Masters insist that a Team reduce its commitments in early Sprints. Successful Teams consistently improve by building on success. Failing Teams stay stuck at low velocity

Product Backlog Refinement

One of the lesser known, but valuable, guidelines in Scrum is that five or ten percent of each Sprint must be dedicated by the Product Owner and the team to refining the Product Backlog.

This includes:
- Detailed requirements analysis
- Splitting large items into smaller ones
- Estimation of new items
- Re-estimation of existing items

A regularly scheduled Weekly meeting with the Product Owner is enough for experienced Teams to refine the Product Backlog. This refinement activity is not for items selected for the current Sprint; it is for items for the future, most likely in the next one or two Sprints. With this practice, Sprint Planning becomes relatively simple because the Product Owner and Scrum Team start the planning with a clear, well analyzed and carefully estimated set of items. A sign that this refinement process is not being done (or not being done well) is that
Sprint Planning involves significant questions, discovery, or confusion.

Ending the Sprint

One of the core tenets of Scrum is that the duration of the Sprint is never extended – it ends on the assigned date regardless of whether the Team has completed the work it committed to. Teams typically over-commit in the first few Sprints and fail to meet objectives. Teams might then overcompensate and under-commit, and finish early. But by the third or fourth Sprint, a Team typically has figured out what it are capable of delivering (most of the time), and it will meet its Sprint goals more reliably after that. Teams are encouraged to pick one duration for Sprints (say, two weeks) and not change it. A consistent duration helps the Team learn how much it can accomplish, which helps in both estimation and longer-term release planning. It also helps the Team achieve a rhythm for their work; this is often referred to as the "heartbeat" of the team in Scrum.

Sprint Review

After the Sprint ends, there is the Sprint Review, where the team reviews the Sprint with the Product Owner. This is often mislabeled the "demo" but that does not capture the real intent of this meeting. A key idea in Scrum is inspect and adapt. To see and learn what is going on and then evolve based on feedback, in repeating cycles. The Sprint Review is an inspect and adapt activity for the product. It is a time for the

Product Owner and key stakeholders to learn what is going on with the product and with the Team (that is, a review of the Sprint); and for the Team to learn what is going on with the Product Owner and the market. Consequently, the most important element of the Review is an in-depth conversation and collaboration between the Team and Product Owner to learn the situation, to get advice, and so forth. The review includes a demo of what the Team built during the Sprint, but if the focus of the review is a demo rather than conversation, there is an
imbalance.

Present at this meeting are the Product Owner, Team members, and Scrum Master, plus customers, stakeholders, experts, executives, and anyone else interested. The demo portion of the Sprint Review is not a "presentation" the team gives – there is no slideware. A guideline in Scrum is that as little time as possible should be spent on preparing for the Sprint Review; Scrum suggests no more than 2 hours. It is simply a demo of what has been built. Anyone present is free to ask questions and give input.

The Sprint Retrospective

The Sprint Review involves inspect and adapt regarding the product. The Sprint Retrospective, which follows the Review, involves inspect and adapt regarding the process.

This is a practice that some teams skip which is unacceptable, because self-organization requires the frequent regular reflection provided by the Retrospective.

It's the main mechanism for taking the visibility that Scrum provides into areas of potential improvement, and turning it into results. It's an opportunity for the entire Scrum Team to discuss what's working and what's not working, and agree on changes to try. Sometimes the

Scrum Master can act as an effective facilitator for the retrospective, but it may be better to find a neutral outsider to facilitate the meeting; a good approach is for Scrum Masters to facilitate each other's retrospectives, which enables cross-pollination among teams.

Updating Release Backlog & Burndown Chart

At this point, some items have been finished, some have been added, some have new estimates, and some have been dropped from the release goal. The Product Owner is responsible for ensuring that these changes are reflected in the Release Backlog (and more broadly, the Product Backlog). In addition, Scrum includes a Release Burndown chart that shows progress towards the release date. It is analogous to the Sprint Burndown chart, but is at the higher level of items (requirements) rather than fine-grained tasks. Since a new Product Owner is unlikely to know why or how to create this chart, this is another opportunity for a Scrum Master to help the Product Owner.

Starting the Next Sprint

Following the Sprint Review, the Product Owner may update the Product Backlog with any new insights. At this point, the Product Owner and Team are ready to begin another Sprint cycle. There is no down time between Sprints – teams normally go from a Sprint Retrospective one afternoon into the next Sprint Planning the following morning (or after the weekend).

One of the principles of agile development is "sustainable pace", and only by working regular hours at a reasonable level can teams continue this cycle indefinitely.

Release Sprint

The perfection vision of Scrum is that the product is potentially shippable at the end of each Sprint, which implies there is no wrap up work required, such as testing or documentation. Rather, the implication is that everything is completely finished every Sprint; that you could actually ship it or deploy it immediately after the Sprint Review.

However, many organizations have weak development practices and cannot achieve this perfection, or there are other extenuating circumstances (such as, "the machine broke"). In this case, there will be some remaining work, such as final production environment integration testing, and so there will be the need for a "Release Sprint" to handle this remaining work. A goal of any Scrum Team is to minimize the number of Release Sprints for completing "undone" work.

Undone work tends to accumulate exponentially and causes poor product quality.

Release Planning & Initial Product Backlog Refinement

A question that is sometimes asked is how, in an iterative model, can long-term release planning be done. There are two cases to consider:
A new product in its first release
An existing product in a later release

In the case of a new product, or an existing product just adopting Scrum, there is the need to do initial Product Backlog refinement before the first Sprint, where the Product Owner and team shape a proper Scrum Product Backlog. This could take a few days or a week, and involves a vision workshop, some detailed requirements analysis, and estimation of all the items identified for the first release.

Surprisingly in Scrum, in the case of an established product with an established Product Backlog, there should not be the need for any special or extensive release planning for the next release. Why?

Because the Product Owner and team should be doing Product Backlog refinement every Sprint (five or ten percent of each Sprint), continuously preparing for the future. This continuous product development mode obviates the need for the dramatic punctuated prepare-execute-conclude stages one sees in traditional sequential life cycle development.

During an initial Product Backlog refinement workshop and during the continuous backlog refinement each Sprint, the Team and Product Owner will do release planning, refining the estimates, priorities, and content as they learn.

Some releases are date-driven; for example: "We will release version 2.0 of our project at a trade-show on November 10." In this situation, the team will complete as many Sprints (and build as many features) as is possible in the time available. Other products require certain features to be built before they can be called complete and the product will not launch until these requirements are satisfied, however long that takes. Since Scrum emphasizes producing potentially shippable code each Sprint, the Product Owner may choose to start doing interim releases, to allow the customer to reap the benefits of completed work sooner.

Since they cannot possibly know everything up front, the focus is on creating and refining a plan to give the release broad direction, and clarify how tradeoff decisions will be made (scope versus schedule, for example). Think of this as the roadmap guiding you towards your final destinations; which exact roads you take and the decisions you make during the journey may be determined en-route.

Most Product Owners choose one release approach.

For example, they will decide a release date, and will work with the team to estimate the Release Backlog items that can be completed by that date. In situations where a "fixed price / fixed date / fixed deliverable" commitment is required – for example, contract development – one or more of those parameters must have a built-in buffer to allow for uncertainty and change; in this respect, Scrum is no different from other approaches. The advantage of Scrum is that new requirements can easily be added into the release at sprint boundaries as long as low priority requirements scheduled later can be removed and still keep the project on time and on budget.

Application or Product Focus

For applications or products – either for the market or for internal use within an organization – Scrum moves groups away from the older project-centric model toward a continuous application/product development model. There is no longer a project with a beginning, middle, and end. And hence no traditional project manager. Rather, there is simply a stable Product Owner and a long-lived self- managing Team that collaborate in an "endless" series of two or four-week Sprints, until the product or application is retired. All necessary "project" management work is handled by the Team and the business owner—who is an internal business customer or from Product Management. It is not managed by an IT manager or someone from a Project Management Office. Scrum can also be used for true projects that are one-time initiatives (rather than work to create or evolve long-lived applications); still, in this case the team and Product Owner do the project management.

What if there is insufficient new work from one or more existing applications to warrant a dedicated long-lived Team for each application? In this case, a stable long-lived Team may take on items from one application in one Sprint, and then items from another in the next Sprint; in this situation the Sprints are often quite short, such as one week.

Occasionally, there is insufficient new work even for this last solution, and the Team may take on items from several applications during the same Sprint; however, beware this solution as it may devolve into unproductive multitasking across multiple applications. A basic productivity theme in Scrum is for the Team to be focused on one product or application for one Sprint.

Common Challenges

Scrum is not only a concrete set of practices – rather, and more importantly, it is a framework that provides visibility to the Team, and a mechanism that allows them to "inspect and adapt" accordingly.

Scrum works by making visible the dysfunction and impediments that are impacting the Product Owner and the Team's effectiveness, so that they can be addressed. For example, the Product Owner may not really know the market, the features, or how to estimate their relative business value. Or the Team may be unskilled in effort estimation or development work.

The Scrum framework will quickly reveal these weaknesses. Scrum does not solve the problems of development; it makes them painfully visible, and provides a framework for people to explore ways to resolve problems in short cycles and with small improvement experiments.

Suppose the team fails to deliver what they committed to in the first Sprint due to poor task analysis and estimation skill. To the team, this feels like failure. But in reality, this experience is the necessary first step toward becoming more realistic and thoughtful about their commitments. This pattern – of Scrum helping make visible dysfunction, enabling the team to do something about it – is the basic mechanism that produces the most significant benefits that teams using Scrum experience.

Another common mistake is to assume that a practice is discouraged or prohibited just because Scrum does not specifically require it. For example, Scrum does not require the Product Owner to set a long term strategy for his or her product; nor does it require engineers to seek advice from more experienced engineers about complex technical problems. Scrum leaves it to the individuals involved to make the right decision; and in most cases, both of these practices (along with many others) are well advised.

Distributed, Outsourced Scrum

US, European, and Japanese companies often outsource software development to Eastern Europe, Russia, or the Far East. Typically, remote teams operate independently and communication problems limit productivity. While there is a large amount of published research on project management, distributed development, and outsourcing strategies as isolated domains, there are few detailed studies of best project management practices on large systems that are both distributed and outsourced.

Distributed Team Models

Here we consider three distributed Scrum models commonly observed in practice:

- **Isolated Scrums** - Teams are isolated across geographies. In most cases off-shore teams are not cross-functional and may not be using the Scrum process.
- **Distributed Scrum of Scrums** – Scrum teams are isolated across geographies and integrated by a Scrum of Scrums that meets regularly across geographies.
- **Totally Integrated Scrums** – Scrum teams are cross- functional with members distributed across geographies.

Most outsourced development efforts use a form of the Isolated Scrums model where outsourced teams are not cross functional and not Agile. Requirements may be created in the UK and developed in Dubai, or development may occur in France and quality assurance in India.

Typically, cross-cultural communication problems are compounded by differences in work style in the primary organization vs. the outsourced group. In the worst case, outsourced teams are not using Scrum and their productivity is typical of waterfall projects further delayed by cross-continent communications lag time.

Best practice recommended by the Scrum Alliance is a Distributed Scrum of Scrums model. This model partitions work across cross functional, isolated Scrum teams while eliminating most dependencies between teams. Scrum teams are linked by a Scrum-of-Scrums where Scrum Masters (team leaders/project managers) meet regularly across locations. This encourages communication, cooperation, and cross fertilization and is appropriate for newcomers to Agile development.

An Integrated Scrums model has all teams fully distributed and each team has members at multiple locations. While this appears to create communication and coordination burdens, the daily Scrum meetings help to break down cultural barriers and disparities in work styles. On large enterprise implementations, it can organize the project into a single whole with an integrated global code base. Proper implementation of this approach provides location transparency and performance characteristics similar to small co-located teams.